Tax Administration Digitalisation and Digital Transformation Initiatives

OECD
BETTER POLICIES FOR BETTER LIVES

Please cite this publication as:
OECD (2025), *Tax Administration Digitalisation and Digital Transformation Initiatives*, OECD Publishing, Paris, https://doi.org/10.1787/c076d776-en.

ISBN 978-92-64-39149-9 (print)
ISBN 978-92-64-98205-5 (PDF)
ISBN 978-92-64-52613-6 (HTML)

Photo credits: Cover © Khanchit Khirisutchalual/Getty images.

Corrigenda to OECD publications may be found at: https://www.oecd.org/en/publications/support/corrigenda.html.

Foreword

Many tax administrations have embarked on a digital transformation journey, introducing new digital initiatives and innovations to support tax compliance and reduce burdens. *Tax Administration Digitalisation and Digital Transformation Initiatives* provides an overview on the extent and progress of the approaches taken by tax administrations. While each may be at a different stage, they share similar goals and common challenges and can learn from one another's experiences.

By summarising the data from the Inventory of Tax Technology Initiatives (OECD et al., 2024[1]), this publication can support tax administrations in considering potential domestic digitalisation and digital transformation reforms. It enables the comparison of efforts, a better understanding of ongoing initiatives and the identification of new approaches. In addition, it helps identify areas where future collaboration between tax administrations could be of most value.

The underlying data was collected through the 2024 Global Survey on Digitalisation which was completed by more than one hundred tax administrations globally. This publication only looks at the data from the 54 members of the OECD Forum on Tax Administration. The data has not been reviewed or validated by the OECD and should be considered as self-reported by the administrations concerned.

This report was approved by the Committee on Fiscal Affairs on 4 June 2025 and prepared for publication by the OECD Secretariat.

Acknowledgements

Tax Administration Digitalisation and Digital Transformation Initiatives summarises data from the Inventory of Tax Technology Initiatives (OECD et al., 2024[1]) which was collected through the 2024 Global Survey on Digitalisation. It would not have been possible without the direct support and help of a large number of people, particularly the staff in the tax administrations that provided the data and reviewed the content that forms the basis of the publication.

The authors of the publication were Oliver Petzold, Fiona May and Peter Green from the OECD's Forum on Tax Administration (FTA) Secretariat. Management and analysis of the data was undertaken by Oliver Petzold. The authors are thankful to Karine Lepron from the OECD's Smart Data Practices and Solutions Division for her work on developing the database that underlies the Inventory of Tax Technology Initiatives. They would also like to thank the work of the wider team at the FTA Secretariat and the OECD Centre for Tax Policy and Administration's Communications team.

Table of contents

FIGURES

TABLES

Reader's guide

Tax administrations covered by this report

Tax Administration Digitalisation and Digital Transformation Initiatives provides an overview on the extent and progress of technology tools and digitalisation solutions implemented by tax administrations. Its primary purpose is to assist tax administrations in their considerations of possible domestic digitalisation and digital transformation reforms as well as to help identify where future collaboration between tax administrations might be of most value, whether bilateral or multilateral.

It summarises the data from the Inventory of Tax Technology Initiatives (OECD et al., 2024[1]) and covers the 54 jurisdictions that are members of the OECD's Forum on Tax Administration (FTA).

The Inventory of Tax Technology Initiatives

The inventory is the result of a global partnership. It has been put together with the assistance of the ISORA Partners (the Inter-American Center of Tax Administrations, the International Monetary Fund, the Intra-European Organisation of Tax Administrations and the OECD), the Asian Development Bank, the African Tax Administration Forum, the Cercle de Reflexion et d'Echange des Dirigeants des Administrations Fiscale, the Commonwealth Association of Tax Administrators, the Pacific Islands Tax Administrators Association and the Study Group on Asia-Pacific Tax Administration and Research.

It is managed by the OECD FTA Secretariat and can be found through the following link: https://www.oecd.org/content/oecd/en/data/datasets/inventory-of-tax-technology-initiatives.html.

Data gathering process

The data underlying the inventory was collected through the 2024 Global Survey on Digitalisation[1] which was launched in April 2024 and completed by more than 100 tax administrations. The data has not been reviewed or validated by the OECD or any of the partner organisations. As a result, all data should be considered as self-reported by the administrations concerned.

Publication structure

The publication is structured around seven chapters: (i) an introduction, followed by chapters on the six building blocks of the OECD's vision for the digital transformation of tax administration, referred to as the Tax Administration 3.0 vision, as described in the OECD publication *Tax Administration 3.0: The Digital Transformation of Tax Administration* (OECD, 2020[2]): (ii) digital identity; (iii) taxpayer touchpoints; (iv) data management and standards; (v) tax rule management and application; (vi) new skill sets; and (vii) governance frameworks.

Forum on Tax Administration

The FTA is a unique body bringing together tax commissioners and tax administration officials from over 50 OECD and non-OECD economies. The FTA is a forum through which tax administrators share knowledge, undertake research and develop new ideas to enhance tax administration around the world. Readers wishing to find out more about the FTA should go to: https://www.oecd.org/en/networks/oecd-forum-on-tax-administration.html. For more information on the OECD's work on tax administration, please visit: https://www.oecd.org/en/topics/tax-administration.html. (Both links accessed on 12 February 2025).

Caveat

Tax administrations operate in varied environments, and the way in which they each administer their taxation system differs in respect to their policy and legislative environment and their administrative practice and culture. As such, a standard approach to tax administration may be neither practical nor desirable in a particular instance. Therefore, this report and the observations it makes need to be interpreted with this in mind. Care should be taken when considering a jurisdiction's practices to fully appreciate the complex factors that have shaped a particular approach. Similarly, regard needs to be had to the distinct challenges and priorities each administration is managing.

Abbreviations and acronyms

APIs	Application Programming Interfaces
AI	Artificial Intelligence
CIT	Corporate Income Tax
DI	Digital Identity
FTA	Forum on Tax Administration
HR	Human Resources
PAYE	Pay-as-you-earn
PIT	Personal Income Tax
TA3.0	Tax Administration 3.0
VAT	Value Added Tax

Executive summary

When the OECD's Forum on Tax Administration (FTA) vision for the future of tax administration – Tax Administration 3.0 – was published in 2020 (OECD, 2020[2]), many tax administrations had already embarked on a digital transformation journey, introducing new digital initiatives and innovations to support tax compliance and reduce burdens. Since then, many more have followed fully embracing the long-term vision and working to make tax become a more seamless experience for citizens and businesses.

Tax Administration Digitalisation and Digital Transformation Initiatives takes a closer look at the extent and progress that tax administrations have made in their digitalisation and digital transformation journeys. Containing a wealth of data, it is intended to be used by tax administration analysts and strategists in their considerations of possible domestic reforms as well as to help them identify where future collaboration might be of most value. While primarily aimed at analysts and strategists, it can also be a useful tool for senior tax administration managers or officials in ministries of finance to understand global trends and to aid them in their considerations of possible future changes in tax system administration.

Using the data from the Inventory of Tax Technology Initiatives (OECD et al., 2024[1]), this report takes a closer look at the technology tools and digitalisation solutions implemented by the 54 members of the FTA. It shows that:

- **Most taxpayers are already using a digital identity** to access online services offered by the tax administration, a prerequisite to provide certainty regarding the identification of taxpayers and to allow systems to interact so that data can be exchanged in real-time.
- **Administrations are integrating tax interactions into third party systems** with more than 80% of tax administrations developing application programming interfaces (APIs), and over three quarters of them making their APIs publicly available for third party use. Some tax administrations have also started creating natural systems for taxpayers as they develop software solutions that taxpayers can use, for example, for record keeping or the creation and conversion of electronic files and forms.
- **Tax administrations increasingly receive data directly from taxpayer business systems and third parties**. Around 80% of administrations reported getting data directly from taxpayer business systems, beyond pay-as-you-earn information, with some data already being sent to the administration automatically from machine-to-machine without human involvement.
- **Many taxpayers enjoy a seamless experience through full prefilling of tax returns**. The majority of administrations is already in a position to offer the complete prefilling of returns for many PIT taxpayers. Thanks to the availability of technology solutions such as electronic invoicing systems, close to 40% of tax administrations also reported being able to prefill VAT returns and around one quarter prefill CIT returns. Around 30% of those are in a position to provide certain VAT and CIT taxpayers with returns that are totally prefilled with no need for taxpayers to make changes.
- **Artificial intelligence (AI) is being used by more than 70% of tax administrations** to enhance effectiveness and efficiency within the administration, for example on compliance management, and to improve taxpayer services. The most common use case is the involvement of AI in the

detection of tax evasion and fraud, followed by the use of AI in risk assessment processes and as part of virtual assistants.

- **Many administrations have started identifying and mapping the skills required for a digital transformation.** Slightly more than a quarter of administrations have identified the future skills required for a successful digital transformation for the whole administration, and an additional 45% have done this for parts of the administration. Of those that do, three quarters collaborate with other government organisations and external partners to improve the staff skills required for digital transformation.
- **Nearly 80% of administrations have developed a digital transformation strategy.** Digital transformation represents a fundamental change in the operating model for an organisation, and to provide for a structured approach, many administrations are increasingly developing digital transformation strategies that set out objectives and plan the timing and priority of the incremental steps. To oversee the relevant processes, provide strategic direction, and ensure the smooth implementation of the digital transformation strategy, close to 80% of administrations have a senior management governance body in place.

The journey to fully digitally transformed tax administration is long and what the data in this report illustrates is that FTA members have already made considerable progress. Given the rapid digital transformation of the wider economy, it will be interesting to see how quickly these changes are progressing within tax administrations when the Inventory of Tax Technology Initiatives and its underlying data is updated in the future.

References

OECD (2020), *Tax Administration 3.0: The Digital Transformation of Tax Administration*, OECD Publishing, Paris, https://doi.org/10.1787/ca274cc5-en. [2]

OECD et al. (2024), *Inventory of Tax Technology Initiatives*, https://www.oecd.org/content/oecd/en/data/datasets/inventory-of-tax-technology-initiatives.html (accessed on 7 February 2025). [1]

Note

[1] The survey can be accessed here: https://www.oecd.org/content/dam/oecd/en/topics/policy-issue-focus/inventory-of-tax-technology-initiatives/global-survey-digitalisation-2024-en.pdf (accessed on 12 February 2025).

1 Introduction

Digital transformation has been an integral part of tax administration in recent years, with administrations increasingly investing resources into reforming their processes to become truly digital. In the context of the digital transformation of wider society, it is imperative that tax administrations keep pace. Technology and digital services have remodelled the way individuals and businesses operate, and tax administrations are adapting to this by fundamentally changing their operating models to benefit from what digital technologies, including the increasing interconnections between digital systems, can now offer.

The heart of the Tax Administration 3.0 vision as described in the OECD's 2020 flagship publication *Tax Administration 3.0: The Digital Transformation of Tax Administration* (OECD, 2020[1]) is the idea that the tax administration of the future will be fully taxpayer-centric, with a focus on how to make taxation a seamless and burden-free process. The different systems and technologies that citizens, businesses and public authorities use – their "natural systems" – are becoming increasingly interconnected. This is now making it more feasible to move taxation processes into taxpayer natural systems where taxable events take place, or are recorded, thus offering opportunities to reduce recording, reporting and calculation burdens.

One of the most important developments has been the rapid evolution of Artificial Intelligence (AI). AI is increasingly being used by tax administrations to improve efficiency and effectiveness within the tax administration on a range of areas, from improving customer services to detecting tax fraud. While AI undoubtedly offers many opportunities, its adoption by tax administrations must be subject to appropriate governance to ensure objectivity, data privacy and trust.

At the heart of the digital transformation process is the staff of the tax administration. The skillsets required by tax administrations are changing, with a greater need for digitally literate staff and people with technical expertise in data management, new technologies and cybersecurity. Project management skills to deliver technical projects and change management skills will also be valuable.

Tax Administration Digitalisation and Digital Transformation Initiatives looks at the progress administrations have made in implementing digital solutions and digital transformation reforms. It does so by analysing the data from the Inventory of Tax Technology Initiatives (OECD et al., 2024[2]), and considering these within the context of the six Tax Administration 3.0 building blocks as illustrated in Figure 1.1.:

- **Digital identity**: As tax administrations are increasingly delivering their services online, digital identity has become a cornerstone of tax administrations' work. Without secure digital identities, it is not possible to move fully to machine-to-machine interactions. ***Chapter 2*** sets out the digital identity services offered by tax administrations, including their usage and key features. It also examines authentication methods and authorisation processes.
- **Taxpayer touchpoints**: Taxpayers have more contact with the tax administration than ever before, especially as administrations offer more online services, often in collaboration with wider government and third parties. This is facilitated through various taxpayer touchpoints, which ***Chapter 3*** looks at in more detail.

Figure 1.1. The Tax Administration 3.0 Building Block Framework

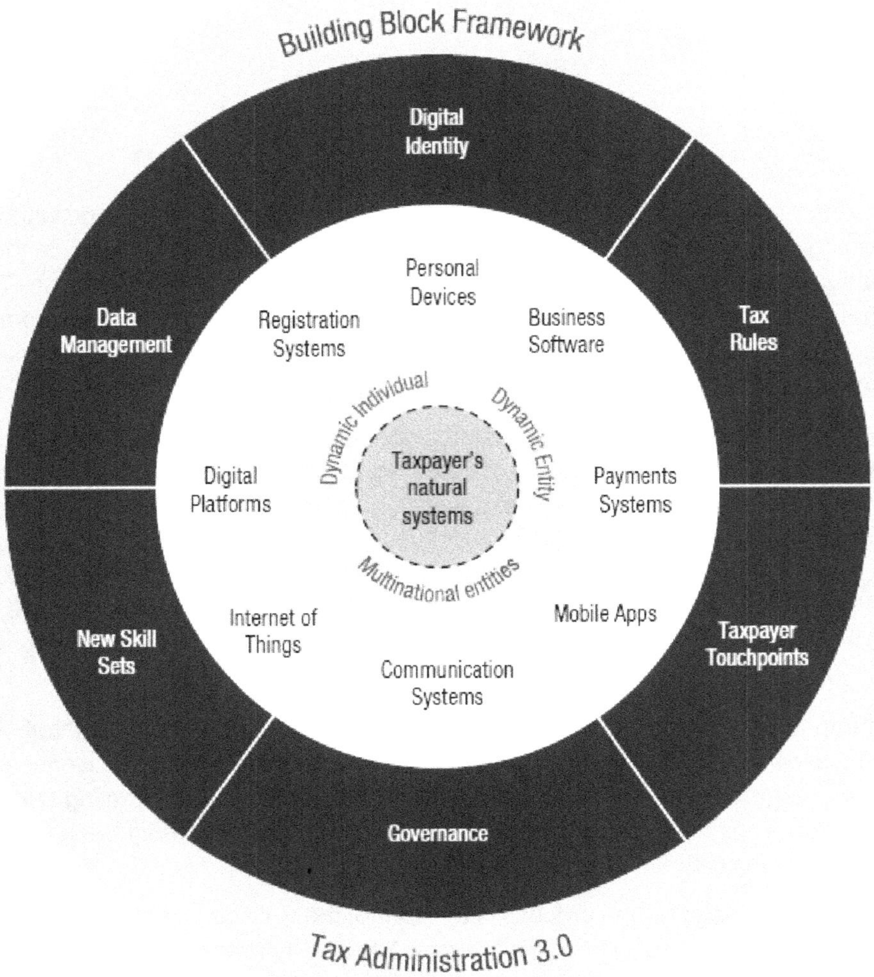

Source: OECD (2020), Tax Administration 3.0: The Digital Transformation of Tax Administration, https://doi.org/10.1787/ca274cc5-en.

- **Data management**: Data is a core part of the effective operation of modern tax administrations and digitalisation is enabling administrations to collect increasing amounts of it. ***Chapter 4*** highlights some of the key considerations in data management, including the importance of data governance, the evolution in how administrations collect data, data sharing, and analytics.
- **Tax rules**: ***Chapter 5*** sets out the advances and innovations in tax rule management. It provides statistics on assurance frameworks, automated registration and deregistration, and third-party withholding taxes. The growing role of AI is also highlighted, alongside considerations for its effective use.
- **New skill sets**: Human resource management and change processes are critical to digital transformation, as new staff will need to be hired, and the skills of existing staff may need to be developed. ***Chapter 6*** looks at the approaches of tax administrations to skill identification and mapping, as well as building a digital culture.
- **Governance**: Finally, ***Chapter 7*** examines the role of governance frameworks in digital transformation, and how having a digital transformation strategy can help tax administrations set out the key objectives, milestones and priorities of the transformation.

References

OECD (2020), *Tax Administration 3.0: The Digital Transformation of Tax Administration*, OECD Publishing, Paris, https://doi.org/10.1787/ca274cc5-en. [1]

OECD et al. (2024), *Inventory of Tax Technology Initiatives*, https://www.oecd.org/content/oecd/en/data/datasets/inventory-of-tax-technology-initiatives.html (accessed on 7 February 2025). [2]

2 Digital identity

Increasingly, engagements between tax administrations and citizens and businesses are happening online which requires a secure and unique identification of all actors involved. Trusted digital identities[1] play a key role as they provide certainty as regards the identification of taxpayers. They give access to online services, allow for the matching of available information and the delegation of representation, and are also instrumental for the provision of joined-up government services and machine-to-machine processes.

This chapter surfaces details around the adoption of digital identities by tax administrations, including their coverage and authentication methods, required for taxpayers to access digital services. It also looks at authorisation processes put in place by tax administrations.

Digital identity usage

Almost all administrations now have digital identity systems in place for individuals and businesses, establishing a strong foundation for digital transformation (see Table 2.1.). The table also shows that it is not necessarily the administration that provides the digital identity. In many jurisdictions the digital identity can be provide by another government body or, in about one third of the jurisdictions, by a private sector body.

The trend is increasingly for these digital identities to enable access to services from other parts of government or third parties. As can be seen in Table 2.1., in more than half of the jurisdictions the digital identity provided by the tax administration can also be used to access services from other government bodies and in around 15% of jurisdictions it can be used to access private sector services.

Table 2.1. Use of digital identities, 2024

Percent of administrations that have the respective process in place

		If yes, ...					
		DI used to access the services can be provided by *(multiple answers possible)*			DIs are interoperable *(if several bodies can provide a DI)*	DI offered by the tax administration can also be used to access services from...	
Taxpayer type	Taxpayers are required to use an approved digital identity (DI) to access secure digital services offered by the administration	Tax administration	Another government body	Private sector body		Another government body	Private sector body
Individual	98.1	71.7	66.0	34.0	67.7	55.3	15.8
Business	96.3	71.2	48.1	36.5	75.0	59.5	13.5

Source: (OECD et al., 2024[1]), Inventory of Tax Technology Initiatives, https://www.oecd.org/content/oecd/en/data/datasets/inventory-of-tax-technology-initiatives.html (accessed on 7 February 2025).

In most jurisdiction it has become the norm to access tax administration services by using an approved digital identity. As Table 2.2. shows, in around two thirds of jurisdictions, between 81% and 100% of individuals use a digital identity to access secure digital services offered by the tax administration. This number is even higher for businesses, with close to 90% of administrations reporting the use of a digital identity by more than 80% of businesses.

Table 2.2. Estimated percentage of the taxpayer population that uses a digital identity to access secure digital services offered by the administration, 2024

Percent of administrations that report a digital identity usage in the respective range

Taxpayer type	Estimated percentage of the taxpayer population that uses an approved DI to access the services				
	0-20 percent	21-40 percent	41-60 percent	61-80 percent	81-100 percent
Individual	0.0	15.1	7.6	11.3	66.0
Business	5.8	1.9	0.0	5.8	86.5

Note: Percentages relate to administrations that require the use of an approved digital identity (see Table 2.1.).
Source: (OECD et al., 2024[1]), Inventory of Tax Technology Initiatives, https://www.oecd.org/content/oecd/en/data/datasets/inventory-of-tax-technology-initiatives.html (accessed on 7 February 2025).

The digital identity solutions offered by tax administrations can have a range of features. As highlighted by Table 2.3., for both individuals and businesses, the majority of these solutions are built upon an existing domestic identity system as opposed to being completely new. Nearly two fifths of digital identify solutions can connect with foreign identity systems, although only 65% of these are already done in practice. In the majority of cases, the digital identity is created on request as opposed to automatically.

Table 2.3. Selected features of the digital identity solution, 2024

Percent of administrations that have the respective process in place

Taxpayer type	Underlying DI solution for is ...		Connection with foreign identity systems			DI is created ...	
				If yes, the connection with foreign identity systems is ...			
	Built upon an existing domestic identity system	Completely new	DI solution can connect with foreign identity systems	Already done in practice	A theoretical possibility	Automatically	On request
Individual	79.2	20.8	37.7	65.0	35.0	17.0	83.0
Business	75.0	25.0	38.5	65.0	35.0	17.3	82.7

Note: Percentages relate to administrations that require the use of an approved digital identity (see Table 2.1.).
Source: (OECD et al., 2024[1]), Inventory of Tax Technology Initiatives, https://www.oecd.org/content/oecd/en/data/datasets/inventory-of-tax-technology-initiatives.html (accessed on 7 February 2025).

Authentication methods

With the significant uptake in the use of digital identities to access online services (as reported in Table 2.2.), it is of utmost importance to have enhanced security systems in place against digital identify theft. It is therefore of no surprise that all administrations report that they apply authentication methods to verify the digital identity when used online.

The type of verification method varies, however, as can be seen in Table 2.4. which shows that password-based authentication is used by 77% of administrations, followed by multi-factor authentication and mobile app. A few administrations are also using facial recognition or fingerprint to authenticate the digital identity of a taxpayer. In addition, two-thirds of the administrations reported that their use of different authentication methods is based on the level of security required for certain types of interactions.

Table 2.4. Digital identity authentication, 2024

Percent of administrations that have the respective process in place

Authentication methods used by the tax administration									Use of different authentication methods based on the level of security required for certain types of interactions
Password-based authentication	ID card	Mobile app	Voice recognition	Facial recognition	Retina scan	Finger-print	Multi-factor authentication	Other	
77.4	39.6	41.5	1.9	17.0	1.9	17.0	69.8	22.6	66.7

Note: Percentages relate to administrations that require the use of an approved digital identity (see Table 2.1.).
Source: (OECD et al., 2024[1]), Inventory of Tax Technology Initiatives, https://www.oecd.org/content/oecd/en/data/datasets/inventory-of-tax-technology-initiatives.html (accessed on 7 February 2025).

Authorisation

Traditionally, many taxpayers are using third parties, such as tax advisors, accountants or intermediaries, to deal with their tax affairs. Close to 90% of tax administrations have therefore put in place processes that allow taxpayers to authorise third parties to access secure digital services on their behalf (see Table 2.5.). Of those that do, almost 90% allow access to be assigned to a named individual, while two thirds allow an entity to be given access.

Table 2.5. Authorisation for accessing secure digital services offered by the tax administration, 2024

Percent of administrations that have the respective process in place

Taxpayers can authorise third parties to access secure digital services	If yes, ...			
	Authorisation can be assigned to ...		Authorised third party can represent ...	
	A named individual	An entity	An individual	An entity
86.8	87.0	65.2	93.5	93.5

Note: Percentages relate to administrations that require the use of an approved digital identity (see Table 2.1.).
Source: (OECD et al., 2024[1]), Inventory of Tax Technology Initiatives, https://www.oecd.org/content/oecd/en/data/datasets/inventory-of-tax-technology-initiatives.html (accessed on 7 February 2025).

Innovations

Addressing security and privacy challenges around the use of digital identities, tax administrations are starting to look into innovative technological approaches. As Table 2.6. shows, close to 10% of administrations indicated using self-sovereign identity approaches that give individuals control of their digital identities, and 14% of administrations reported using a digital identity wallet solution where identity data and official documents are stored and managed. Around 6% of administration reported the use of artificial intelligence as part of the digital identity system, while none have reported the use of blockchain.

Table 2.6. Use of innovative technologies or solutions with respect to digital identity, 2024

Percent of administrations that have the respective process in place

Type of technology or solution used			
Blockchain	Self-sovereign identity	Digital identity wallet solution	Artificial intelligence
0.0	9.4	13.5	5.7

Note: Percentages relate to administrations that require the use of an approved digital identity (see Table 2.1.).
Source: (OECD et al., 2024[1]), Inventory of Tax Technology Initiatives, https://www.oecd.org/content/oecd/en/data/datasets/inventory-of-tax-technology-initiatives.html (accessed on 7 February 2025).

Additional information on the use of digital identities within tax administration, such as on the different domestic solutions adopted as well as the challenges related to cross-border processes, can be found in the OECD report *Tax Administration 3.0 and the Digital Identification of Taxpayers: Initial Findings* (OECD, 2022[2]).

References

OECD (2022), *Tax Administration 3.0 and the Digital Identification of Taxpayers: Initial Findings*, OECD Publishing, Paris, https://doi.org/10.1787/3ab1789a-en. [2]

OECD et al. (2024), *Inventory of Tax Technology Initiatives*, https://www.oecd.org/content/oecd/en/data/datasets/inventory-of-tax-technology-initiatives.html (accessed on 7 February 2025). [1]

Note

[1] For the purpose of the survey underlying the Inventory of Tax Technology Initiatives (OECD et al., 2024[1]), digital identity is considered to be an electronic representation of an individual or business which enables them to be sufficiently distinguished when interacting online. The digital identity includes attributes which are bound to a credential that is used to authenticate the individual or business.

3 Taxpayer touchpoints

Taxpayer touchpoints facilitate the engagement between taxpayers and the tax administration. They are necessary to effectively and efficiently run a tax system and to address friction where it arises. On their journey to implement the vision of Tax Administration 3.0 (OECD, 2020[1]), tax administrations will strive to eliminate as much friction as possible to build a seamless tax system. However, where friction cannot be eliminated, taxpayer touchpoints will continue to play an important role. As part of this, tax administrations will look to provide real-time services, including automated responses to taxpayer enquiries, and they will try to identify opportunities to move touchpoints into taxpayers' natural systems.

This chapter comments on some of the developments as regards taxpayer touchpoints. Amongst other things, it looks at the online services offered by tax administrations and how they use technology during taxpayer interactions, including artificial intelligence. It also examines the progress made as to embedding touchpoints into the natural systems used by taxpayers, for example, through the use of application programming interfaces.

Online services

The past years have seen an increasing demand for digital service channels and an emphasis on more personalised services. Tax administrations have responded to this by expanding the range of digital services on offer. This is beneficial to the taxpayer because it promotes more self-service, enables a more 24/7 style of service, and reduces waiting times for assistance. From a tax administration point of view, it can increase the automation of services, which reduces administrative costs and increases efficiency.

Services offering

A central component of supporting taxpayer compliance is the supply of a wide range of effective and user-friendly services for taxpayers. Table 3.1. provides an overview of selected online services offered by tax administrations for the three main tax types. It shows that the vast majority of tax administrations offer online many of the interactions between them and taxpayers.

As can be seen in Table 3.1., services such as registering for tax, filing tax returns, making tax payments, filing tax related objections, dealing with correspondence, and uploading data, are now offered online by around 90% or more of the administrations. In addition, approximately three quarters of administrations offer the ability to ask for tax payment arrangements and to make confidential enquiries.

Out of the selected services shown in Table 3.1., only the requesting of extensions of filing or payment deadlines is lagging behind the other service offerings, with around 60% of tax administrations allowing taxpayers to ask for such extensions online.

Table 3.1. Online services offered by tax administrations by tax type, 2024

Percent of administrations that have the respective process in place

Interaction type	Personal income tax	Corporate income tax	Value added tax
Registering for tax	88.5	87.0	92.0
Filing tax returns	100.0	98.1	100.0
Making tax payments	90.4	92.6	92.0
Requesting extensions of deadlines (filing and payment)	65.4	61.1	60.0
Asking for tax payment arrangements	75.0	72.2	76.0
Asking confidential enquiries in a secure environment	75.0	74.1	74.0
Filing tax related objections	88.5	77.8	84.0
Dealing with correspondence	90.4	88.9	90.0
Uploading data into the tax administration's systems	86.5	87.0	86.0

Source: (OECD et al., 2024[2]), Inventory of Tax Technology Initiatives, https://www.oecd.org/content/oecd/en/data/datasets/inventory-of-tax-technology-initiatives.html (accessed on 7 February 2025).

As the online services offered by tax administrations increase, administrations are recognising that for some of these services there might be opportunities to collaborate with other government agencies to provide a whole of government experience.

Table 3.2. shows that for roughly 40% of jurisdictions, making tax payments is part of a wider government online payment portal. In addition, for two thirds of jurisdictions, registration for corporate income tax (CIT) is part of a wider government online registration approach, and roughly half of jurisdictions do the same for personal income tax (PIT) and value added tax (VAT).

Table 3.2. Tax related services as part of a wider government service approach by tax type, 2024

Percent of jurisdictions where the respective tax process is part of a wider government service approach

Interaction type	Personal income tax	Corporate income tax	Value added tax
Registration for tax is part of a wider government online registration approach	50.0	66.7	48.0
Making tax payments is part of a wider government online payment portal	40.4	40.7	42.0

Source: (OECD et al., 2024[2]), Inventory of Tax Technology Initiatives, https://www.oecd.org/content/oecd/en/data/datasets/inventory-of-tax-technology-initiatives.html (accessed on 7 February 2025).

To increase efficiency and reduce administrative costs, many tax administrations are also increasingly automating their online services. As Table 3.3. demonstrates, there are a range of online services for which tax administrations are now fully automating responses (when pre-determined criteria are met).

Table 3.3. Online services with automated responses by tax type, 2024

Percent of administrations that provide automated responses (when pre-determined criteria are met) without human intervention

Interaction type	Personal income tax	Corporate income tax	Value added tax
Registering for tax: Registrant receives automated response with the tax registration number	69.2	70.4	56.0
Filing tax returns: Returns are automatically processed and assessments sent to taxpayers	76.9	64.8	74.0
Making payments: Payments are instantaneously processed and reflected in balances visible to the taxpayer	46.2	51.9	52.0
Requesting extensions of deadlines: Requesting person receives automated response whether request has been accepted or rejected	26.9	22.2	22.0
Asking for tax payment arrangements: Requesting person receives automated response whether request has been accepted or rejected	48.1	44.4	42.0

Source: (OECD et al., 2024[2]), Inventory of Tax Technology Initiatives, https://www.oecd.org/content/oecd/en/data/datasets/inventory-of-tax-technology-initiatives.html (accessed on 7 February 2025).

Use of technology during taxpayer interactions

In order to improve the taxpayer experience and the value of service offerings, tax administrations are increasingly supporting their static online content (for example, web pages and guidance notes) with interactive online services. To support this shift, tax administrations are increasingly leveraging technology during interactions with taxpayers to provide comprehensive, real-time and easily accessible assistance to them.

Virtual assistants

The use of virtual or digital assistants to help answer taxpayer questions and support self-service is common, as demonstrated by Table 3.4. which shows that nearly three quarters of administrations indicate having virtual assistants, such as chatbots. Nearly all of these administrations have virtual assistants that follow a set of pre-programmed rules during interactions with taxpayers. However, 28% of administrations are also using artificial intelligence (AI) in their virtual assistants to deliver more sophisticated levels of support. This can allow the system to cope with more complex questions being asked by taxpayers and/or more personalised answers being given. These systems also have the ability to self-improve over time.

Table 3.4. Availability of virtual assistants, 2024

Percent of administrations that have the respective process in place

	If yes, ...	
Virtual assistant(s), such as chatbots, are available	Virtual assistant(s) follows a set of pre-programmed rules during interactions with taxpayers	Virtual assistant(s) uses other artificial intelligence to personalise interactions with taxpayers
74.1	97.5	27.5

Source: (OECD et al., 2024[2]), Inventory of Tax Technology Initiatives, https://www.oecd.org/content/oecd/en/data/datasets/inventory-of-tax-technology-initiatives.html (accessed on 7 February 2025).

Artificial intelligence

Artificial intelligence is starting to be used not only for powering virtual assistants, but also in other interactions with taxpayers, for example, to provide guidance to taxpayers as well as to assist tax officials. Just over a fifth of administrations use AI during such interactions, as can be seen in Table 3.5. This includes the use of AI to assist taxpayers during the filing of tax returns, to suggest potential responses to tax officials while dealing with incoming correspondence, or to assist tax officials during live chats with taxpayers.

Table 3.5. Use of AI during interactions with taxpayers (other than virtual assistants), 2024

Percent of administrations that have the respective process in place

AI is used during interactions with taxpayers (other than virtual assistants)	If yes, type of interaction ...			
	To suggest potential responses for incoming correspondence	To assist tax officials during live chats with taxpayers	To assist taxpayers during the filing of returns	Other interactions
22.2	25.0	25.0	33.3	50.0

Source: (OECD et al., 2024[2]), Inventory of Tax Technology Initiatives https://www.oecd.org/content/oecd/en/data/datasets/inventory-of-tax-technology-initiatives.html (accessed on 7 February 2025).

Pre-programmed and automated service responses

The use of pre-programmed and automated service responses can reduce burdens for the administration and reduce costs, while at the same time manage high volume of inquiries in a consistent and accurate manner throughout the day. As illustrated in Table 3.6. around two-thirds of administrations offer services that follow a set of pre-programmed and automated responses during interactions with taxpayers, with most of them doing this as part of telephone services or return filing services.

Table 3.6. Pre-programmed and automated service responses during interactions with taxpayers (other than virtual assistants), 2024

Percent of administrations that have the respective process in place

Administration offers services that follow a set of pre-programmed and automated service responses during interactions with taxpayers (other than virtual assistants)	If yes, type of service ...				
	Telephone services, such as interactive voice response (IVR) systems	Return filing services	Taxpayer registration services	Payment services	Other services
68.5	64.9	54.1	32.4	29.7	32.4

Source: (OECD et al., 2024[2]), Inventory of Tax Technology Initiatives https://www.oecd.org/content/oecd/en/data/datasets/inventory-of-tax-technology-initiatives.html (accessed on 7 February 2025).

Ensuring accessibility

Tax administrations need to consider that some citizens may not be able to access online services, for example, because they have no access to internet or are less able to use available online tools. Ensuring accessibility through offline service options, alternative formats, or the use of certain design practices, such as screen reader compatibility or text-to-speech options, can help bridge communication gaps and improves access to tax services. These efforts can help to strengthen trust in the tax system and support voluntary compliance.

Although the trend is increasingly for tax administrations to offer its services online, most also take measures to ensure that they remain accessible for taxpayers who are not able to communicate via the internet. Table 3.7. shows that 87% of administrations offer specific approaches to those that do not have online access. In addition, over three quarters of administrations ensure that online services are available to citizens who have visual, auditory, motor or cognitive disabilities, and 63% of those administrations measure how those taxpayers perceive the quality of the service offerings.

Table 3.7. Ensuring accessibility, 2024

Percent of administrations that have the respective process in place

Administration offers specific approaches to those that do not have online access	Taxpayers who have visual, auditory, motor or cognitive disabilities: Administration ensures that its online services are available to a wide range of users including those users who have visual, auditory, motor or cognitive disabilities	Taxpayers who have visual, auditory, motor or cognitive disabilities: If yes, administration measures how those taxpayers perceive the quality of the service offerings
87.0	75.9	63.4

Source: (OECD et al., 2024[2]), Inventory of Tax Technology Initiatives, https://www.oecd.org/content/oecd/en/data/datasets/inventory-of-tax-technology-initiatives.html (accessed on 7 February 2025).

Measuring taxpayer experience

Given the increased focus of tax administrations on providing online services, most administrations measure taxpayer experience in order to help in identifying issues of concern, improving quality, and increasing user satisfaction. It can also provide insights into gaps in service provision and new service expectations. As highlighted in Table 3.8., 91% of administrations measure taxpayer experiences in using online service. Of those that do this, surveys are the most popular tool to use, followed by online feedback channels. Just over half carry out user testing and web analytics, while just under half conduct interviews.

Table 3.8. Measuring taxpayer experience in using online services, 2024

Percent of administrations that have the respective process in place

Administration measures taxpayer experience in using online services	If yes, approach used...					
	Survey (online or paper)	Online feedback channels (other than survey)	User testing	Web analytics	Interview (phone or in-person)	Other
90.7	89.8	71.4	55.1	53.1	49.0	8.2

Source: (OECD et al., 2024[2]), Inventory of Tax Technology Initiatives, https://www.oecd.org/content/oecd/en/data/datasets/inventory-of-tax-technology-initiatives.html (accessed on 7 February 2025).

Embedding services in taxpayer's natural systems

By embedding services and processes in the natural systems used by citizens and businesses as part of their daily interactions, taxpayers can more easily comply with tax requirements in a seamless manner, and experience reduced administrative burdens and fewer data entry errors. Most of those natural systems are prepared by third-party software developers and many administrations are driving collaboration with those developers to open up new services, including pre-filling.

Integrating tax interactions into third party systems

The connection between the tax administration's system and the natural systems of taxpayers is typically facilitated through Application Programming Interfaces (APIs) which allow a connectivity between systems without providing direct access. Table 3.9. shows that more than 80% of tax administrations are developing APIs, with over three quarters of them making their APIs publicly available for third party use. Further, as part of the process of developing APIs, more than half of tax administrations are engaging in co-creation with third parties.

Table 3.9. Development of APIs, 2024

Percent of administrations that have the respective process in place

Administration develops APIs	If yes, ... Administration makes a library of APIs publicly available for third party use	Administration engages in co-creation of APIs with third parties
83.3	75.6	55.6

Source: (OECD et al., 2024[2]), Inventory of Tax Technology Initiatives, https://www.oecd.org/content/oecd/en/data/datasets/inventory-of-tax-technology-initiatives.html (accessed on 7 February 2025).

Table 3.10. illustrates for which type of interactions tax administrations have published APIs. The most common APIs are published for filing tax returns, for uploading data into the tax administration's systems, for making tax payments, for registering for tax, and for dealing with correspondence.

Table 3.10. Interactions for which administrations have published APIs by tax type, 2024

Percent of administrations that have the respective process in place

Interaction type	Personal income tax	Corporate income tax	Value added tax
Registering for tax	34.1	35.6	30.2
Filing tax returns	59.1	64.4	65.1
Making tax payments	40.9	37.8	37.2
Requesting extensions of deadlines (filing and payment)	15.9	13.3	11.6
Asking for tax payment arrangements	11.4	11.1	16.3
Asking confidential enquiries in a secure environment	22.7	22.2	23.3
Filing tax related objections	15.9	15.6	18.6
Dealing with correspondence	31.8	33.3	30.2
Uploading data into the tax administration's systems	54.5	51.1	51.2
Other interactions	34.1	37.8	44.2

Source: (OECD et al., 2024[2]), Inventory of Tax Technology Initiatives, https://www.oecd.org/content/oecd/en/data/datasets/inventory-of-tax-technology-initiatives.html (accessed on 7 February 2025).

The OECD report *Unlocking the Digital Economy: A Guide to Unlocking Application Programming Interfaces in Government* (OECD, 2019[3]) provides an overview of the practices, techniques and standards used to deliver services for taxpayers through APIs. In addition, reports in the OECD's Tax Administration Series contain numerous examples of API developments in tax administration, see *Tax Administration 2024* (OECD, 2024[4]) and previous editions.

In addition, the 2022 OECD report *Towards Seamless Taxation: Supporting SMEs to Get Tax Right* (OECD, 2022[5]) examines how tax administrations are working to integrate taxation processes into SME taxpayers' natural systems and identifies some of the key benefits and considerations.

Creating software packages for use by taxpayers

In addition to embedding services, some tax administrations have also started creating natural systems for taxpayers by developing software solutions that taxpayers can use, for example, for record keeping, the creation and conversion of electronic files and forms, and the pre-filling of returns. These software products may provide guidance, enhance accessibility, allow for a better integration between IT systems, and thus help reduce errors and improve compliance, while also reducing burdens.

As can be seen in Table 3.11., tax administrations can do this by themselves or in partnership with third parties. The most common software solutions created by tax administrations either by themselves or in commercial partnerships with third parties relate to return-filing processes, followed by solutions for electronic invoicing purposes.

Table 3.11. (Co-)creation of software packages, 2024

Percent of administrations that have the respective process in place

	Types of software				
Development approach	Bookkeeping and accounting software	Payroll software	Invoicing software	Return-filing software	Other software
Software created by the administration	16.7	16.7	35.2	48.1	33.3
Software for which the administration engages in commercial partnerships with third parties	20.4	18.5	25.9	31.5	27.8

Source: (OECD et al., 2024[2]), Inventory of Tax Technology Initiatives, https://www.oecd.org/content/oecd/en/data/datasets/inventory-of-tax-technology-initiatives.html (accessed on 7 February 2025).

References

OECD (2024), *Tax Administration 2024: Comparative Information on OECD and other Advanced and Emerging Economies*, OECD Publishing, Paris, https://doi.org/10.1787/2d5fba9c-en. [4]

OECD (2022), *Towards Seamless Taxation: Supporting SMEs to Get Tax Right*, OECD Publishing, Paris, https://doi.org/10.1787/656c89ab-en. [5]

OECD (2020), *Tax Administration 3.0: The Digital Transformation of Tax Administration*, OECD Publishing, Paris, https://doi.org/10.1787/ca274cc5-en. [1]

OECD (2019), *Unlocking the Digital Economy: A Guide to Implementing Application Programming Interfaces in Government*, OECD Publishing, Paris, https://doi.org/10.1787/56697aa7-en. [3]

OECD et al. (2024), *Inventory of Tax Technology Initiatives*, https://www.oecd.org/content/oecd/en/data/datasets/inventory-of-tax-technology-initiatives.html (accessed on 7 February 2025). [2]

4 Data management and standards

Data plays a central role in modern tax administrations, facilitating effective tax collection, compliance enforcement, and informed decision making. Increasing volumes of data are being handled by tax administrations as they transform into data-driven organisations. While the location of this data becomes less relevant under the Tax Administration 3.0 vision (OECD, 2020[1]), it still requires the application of mechanisms to manage and to protect data.

As shown in Table 4.1., around three quarters of tax administrations have a comprehensive data management strategy, and this chapter looks at some of the underlying mechanisms put in place by tax administrations covering data governance, data collection, data sharing and data analytics.

Data governance

The increasing volumes of data being handled by tax administrations has also been accompanied by the development and the application of more sophisticated approaches to protect and manage data and ensure data confidentiality, helping to uphold taxpayer trust in the system while ensuring compliance with legal obligations.

Alongside the digitalisation of tax administrations, there is an increased role for data analytics and AI-driven automation, which can assist tax administrations in modernising processes such as the pre-filling of tax returns, data sharing and withholding tax calculations as well as the wider provision of digital taxpayer services.

Data confidentiality and security, as well as enhanced data quality standards, also underpins the effective and secure exchange of information within jurisdictions, including with third parties, as well as between governments, helping ensure that all parties have trust in the exchange frameworks.

Data governance lies at the centre of data management as it ensures the availability, quality and security of data, and thus helps upholding taxpayer trust in the system. With the amount of incoming data and its use expanding, tax administrations are investing into data governance processes and safeguards to ensure that the data is stored and used appropriately and well protected, internally as well as externally.

Table 4.1. takes a closer look at some of the data governance practices applied by tax administrations around:

- **Data quality**: The importance of data quality cannot be overstated. Having accurate, complete and timely data is a necessity for any tax administration. In this respect, it is good to see that 85% of administrations assess the quality of reported data.
- **Data access and security**: Protecting data from unauthorised access is a key priority for tax administrations as data breaches, internally and externally, can undermine trust in the wider tax system. Nearly all administrations control user data access and security, and 94% have both cyber security units and hire external parties to test the security of systems. Moreover, 87% of administrations have systems in place that automatically detect unauthorised data access, and 85% employ a Data Privacy Officer.

- **Data ethics**: Three quarters of administrations report having in place a data ethics framework to guide the appropriate and responsible use of data.

Already 17% of administrations report having started using artificial intelligence as part of their data governance, something that is likely to grow quickly.

Table 4.1. Data governance, 2024

Percent of administrations that have the respective process in place

Comprehensive data management strategy exists	Quality of reported data is assessed	Data ethics framework in place	User data access and security is controlled	Unauthorised access is automatically detected	Data Privacy Officer is employed	Cyber security unit exists	External parties hired to test the security of systems	Artificial intelligence used as part of the data governance process
72.2	85.2	75.9	98.1	87.0	85.2	94.4	94.4	16.7

Source: (OECD et al., 2024[2]), Inventory of Tax Technology Initiatives, https://www.oecd.org/content/oecd/en/data/datasets/inventory-of-tax-technology-initiatives.html (accessed on 7 February 2025).

Data collection

Receiving data from taxpayer business systems and third parties

With more and more data becoming available in electronic format, the access, transfer and integration of data has also changed. Instead of taxpayers having to process data and put it in paper or online forms, tax administrations increasingly receive data directly from taxpayer business systems and third parties. This requires effective collaboration with third parties to ensure that the systems are accurate, secure and operate smoothly. Application programming interfaces (APIs) are playing a greater role in this, as seen in Chapter 3, but there are also now mechanisms that allow administrations to access the data directly in the taxpayer natural systems.

As part of pay-as-you-earn (PAYE) systems tax administrations have received data directly from employer business systems since many years. As Table 4.2. highlights, for around 80% of administrations this is now also the case for other data beyond PAYE. Of those that receive such data, 93% of administrations indicated that some data can be uploaded manually onto the administration's systems, and for 77% some data can be sent to the administration automatically from machine-to-machine without human involvement.

Additionally, 89% of administrations reporting receiving data directly from third parties. Again, nearly all administrations reported that some of this data can be uploaded manually onto the administration's systems via dedicated interfaces, and for 79% some data can be sent to the administration automatically from machine-to-machine.

Finally, a small number of administrations (15%) indicated that they can routinely access data stored in taxpayer natural systems, underlining the importance of trust between taxpayers and the tax administration.

Table 4.2. Receiving data from taxpayer business systems and third parties, 2024

Percent of administrations that have the respective process in place

	If yes, ...			If yes, ...		
Administration receives data directly from taxpayer business systems (beyond PAYE systems)	Some data can be sent to the administration automatically from machine-to-machine without human involvement	Some data can be uploaded manually onto the administration's systems via dedicated interfaces	Administration receives data directly from third parties	Some data can be sent to the administration automatically from machine-to-machine without human involvement	Some data can be uploaded manually onto the administration's systems via dedicated interfaces	Administration's IT system can routinely access data stored in taxpayer natural systems
81.5	77.3	93.2	88.9	79.2	95.8	14.8

Source: (OECD et al., 2024[2]), Inventory of Tax Technology Initiatives, https://www.oecd.org/content/oecd/en/data/datasets/inventory-of-tax-technology-initiatives.html (accessed on 7 February 2025).

The OECD report *Tax Administration 3.0 and Connecting with Natural Systems: Initial Findings* (OECD, 2022[3]) examines the issues and challenges related to moving towards connected data systems, and explores the issues that stem from managing the availability, quality and accuracy of data that is drawn remotely from taxpayers' natural systems.

Use of data for return prefilling

One of the most significant evolutions in the tax return process in recent years has been the development of prefilled tax returns reducing compliance burdens and costs for taxpayers. The prefilled approach entails administrations 'prepopulating' the taxpayer's return with information from third parties. This can then be reviewed by the taxpayer and either filed electronically or in paper format. What started in relation to personal income tax (PIT) returns has now, thanks to the availability of technology solutions such as electronic invoicing systems,[1] also become available for other taxes, such as value-added tax (VAT) and corporate income tax (CIT).

Prefilled returns are particularly common for PIT, as shown in Table 4.3., where 85% of administrations prefill PIT returns with the data that they have collected. Of those that do, 75% indicated that they are able to prefill PIT returns with all necessary data so that taxpayers do not need to make any changes.

With more data being available, close to 40% of tax administrations reported being able to prefill VAT returns and around 25% reported being able to prefill CIT returns. Around 30% of those are in a position to provide VAT and CIT taxpayers with returns that are totally prefilled with no need for taxpayers to make changes.

The OECD Tax Administration publications, such as the 2024 edition (OECD, 2024[4]), contain more detailed information on this topic, including a large number of examples of prefilling developments in jurisdictions.

Table 4.3. Prefilling tax returns by tax type, 2024

Percent of administrations that have the respective process in place

Prefilling approach		Personal income tax	Corporate income tax	Value added tax
Administration automatically prefills tax returns with data that it has collected		84.6	25.9	38.0
If yes, ...	Returns are automatically prefilled with income information (For VAT: with information on sales transactions and output VAT)	97.7	78.6	89.5
	Returns are automatically prefilled with expense/allowance information (For VAT: with information on purchase transactions and input VAT)	77.3	71.4	89.5
	For certain taxpayers, the administration prefills tax returns with all necessary data so that they do not need to change the return	75.0	28.6	31.6

Source: (OECD et al., 2024[2]), Inventory of Tax Technology Initiatives, https://www.oecd.org/content/oecd/en/data/datasets/inventory-of-tax-technology-initiatives.html (accessed on 7 February 2025).

To enable the prefilling of information, some jurisdictions are simplifying their tax rules. Table 4.4. shows that 46% of jurisdictions currently do this, with a variation of approaches taken to simplify the rules. For example, over half have simplified or reduced the number of taxable deductions/allowances, and 47% have created special tax regimes with simplified rules for calculating income.

Table 4.4. Simplified tax rules to allow for the prefilling of returns with all necessary data, 2024

Percent of jurisdictions that have taken the respective approach

Jurisdiction simplified tax rules to allow for the prefilling of returns with all necessary data	Approach taken to simplify the tax rule		
	Simplification or reduction of number of taxable deductions / allowances	Creation of special tax regimes with simplified rules for calculating income	Other approaches
45.5	53.3	46.7	53.3

Source: (OECD et al., 2024[2]), Inventory of Tax Technology Initiatives, https://www.oecd.org/content/oecd/en/data/datasets/inventory-of-tax-technology-initiatives.html (accessed on 7 February 2025).

The extent to which a return can be prefilled is generally determined by the range of electronic data available to the administration, which comes from a variety of third-party data providers. Table 4.5. highlights that other government entities are the most common source of data (80%), closely followed by banks and insurance companies (76%).

Table 4.5. Providers of data used to prefill tax returns, 2024

Percent of administrations that receive the respective data

Online marketplaces (incl. sharing and gig economy)	Other online platforms, e.g. stock trading, currencies (incl. crypto)	Taxpayer accounting systems	E-invoicing systems	Online cash registers	Other government entities	Private entities such as banks and insurance companies	Other jurisdictions (beyond data received under CRS, FATCA and DAC)
42.2	40.0	48.9	37.8	24.4	80.0	75.6	31.1

Source: (OECD et al., 2024[2]), Inventory of Tax Technology Initiatives, https://www.oecd.org/content/oecd/en/data/datasets/inventory-of-tax-technology-initiatives.html (accessed on 7 February 2025).

Data sharing

Data sharing internally, within government, and with third parties is an important aspect of digital transformation, reducing burdens on taxpayers and citizens and allowing both taxation processes and other government processes to become more seamless over time.

Many governments are moving towards implementing the once-only principle, meaning that stakeholders supply data only once to one public administration body from where it can then be shared among other government agencies and reused for multiple purposes. Tax administrations have a crucial role to play within government in this regard, as they tend to hold up-to-date information on identity and accounts, are involved in payments, and have mechanisms in place to exchange significant amounts of information with third parties.

Data sharing internally and within government

For many tax administrations the 'collect once, use many times' approach starts internally with close to 90% of them having an enterprise data management system that allows taxpayer information to be viewed across the administration. Table 4.6. also shows that nearly all administrations share bulk information with other government agencies (or even provide them with direct access to information), and receive bulk information from other government agencies or have direct access.

Moving away from data silos both within and across government agencies will significantly reduce burdens and will enable taxation processes and other government procedures to become more seamless for citizens and businesses.

Table 4.6. Data sharing internally and within government, 2024

Percent of administrations that have the respective process in place

Enterprise data management system that allows taxpayer information to be viewed across the administration exists	Sharing data with other parts of government	
	Administration shares bulk information with other government agencies or provides them with direct access to information	Administration receives bulk information from other government agencies or has direct access to information other government agencies hold
88.9	96.3	96.3

Source: (OECD et al., 2024[2]), Inventory of Tax Technology Initiatives, https://www.oecd.org/content/oecd/en/data/datasets/inventory-of-tax-technology-initiatives.html (accessed on 7 February 2025).

Beyond information sharing among public agencies, three quarters of jurisdictions have started developing common cross government databases (see Table 4.7.). This simplifies data access and ensures that public agencies have up-to-date information, with citizens and businesses only needing to provide the data once. As can be seen in Table 4.7., the most common databases are population register, property register, business register and motor vehicle register.

Table 4.7. Common cross government databases, 2024

Percent of jurisdictions that have the respective process in place

Common cross government databases exist	If yes, types of databases				
	Population register	Property register	Business register	Motor vehicle register	Other
75.9	82.9	80.5	85.4	75.6	46.3

Source: (OECD et al., 2024[2]), Inventory of Tax Technology Initiatives, https://www.oecd.org/content/oecd/en/data/datasets/inventory-of-tax-technology-initiatives.html (accessed on 7 February 2025).

Data sharing with non-government third parties

In addition to sharing data within government, administrations are also increasingly sharing individual taxpayer data with non-government third parties, for example, to improve the collection of withholding taxes. As set out in Table 4.8., nearly half of the administrations share data with tax intermediaries, and close to 40% share information with financial institutions. The table also shows that it varies on the third-party type as to whether this data sharing is done automatically, or if data sharing is initiated by the taxpayer.

Table 4.8. Data sharing with non-government third parties, 2024

Percent of administrations that have the respective process in place

		If yes, ...	
Third-party type	Individual taxpayer data shared	Data sharing is done automatically	Data sharing is initiated by the taxpayer
Employers	29.6	81.3	56.3
Withholding agents	29.6	68.8	31.3
Tax intermediaries	48.1	34.6	76.9
Financial institutions	38.9	71.4	61.9
Other third parties	22.2	75.0	41.7

Source: (OECD et al., 2024[2]), Inventory of Tax Technology Initiatives, https://www.oecd.org/content/oecd/en/data/datasets/inventory-of-tax-technology-initiatives.html (accessed on 7 February 2025).

With tax administrations holding vast amounts of structured data, it is no surprise that certain stakeholders have an interest to access such information for analytical purposes, such as for research and statistical projects. To protect taxpayer privacy and confidentiality such data is anonymised.

As illustrated in Table 4.9., around two thirds of administrations share anonymised taxpayer data on a confidential basis with third parties for analytical purposes. In terms of the type of third party that this data is shared with, statistics offices are the most common at 86%, while 60% share with academic/research institutions. In addition, 29% of administrations share with the central/national bank, and 26% share with international organisations.

Table 4.9. Data sharing with third parties for analytical purposes, 2024

Percent of administrations that have the respective process in place

Anonymised taxpayer data shared on a confidential basis with third parties for analytical purposes	If yes, types of third parties that received anonymised taxpayer data				
	Statistics office(s)	Central / national bank	International organisations	Academic / research institutions	Other
64.8	85.7	28.6	25.7	60.0	31.4

Source: (OECD et al., 2024[2]), Inventory of Tax Technology Initiatives, https://www.oecd.org/content/oecd/en/data/datasets/inventory-of-tax-technology-initiatives.html (accessed on 7 February 2025).

Data analytics

Data analytics has become an essential and integrated part of tax administration, supporting both operational functions and the discovery of new opportunities for enhanced efficiency and effectiveness in helping the administration to fulfil its objectives. It can help detect and prevent tax fraud by identifying patterns or anomalies in taxpayer behaviour and, as can be seen in Table 4.10., slightly more than half of the administrations use the analytics function to do those things in real-time.

Table 4.10. Data analytics: Selected features, 2024

Percent of administrations that have the respective process in place

Big data capabilities with the necessary people, skills and infrastructure exist	An enterprise-wide Business Intelligence and Visualisation tool is used	Analytics used for real-time tax fraud detection and prevention
85.2	88.9	51.9

Source: (OECD et al., 2024[2]), Inventory of Tax Technology Initiatives, https://www.oecd.org/content/oecd/en/data/datasets/inventory-of-tax-technology-initiatives.html (accessed on 7 February 2025).

With vast amounts of structured and unstructured information in the hands of tax administrations, an important element for success is the availability of the necessary capabilities. Around 85% of administrations indicated that they have the required people, skills and infrastructure to analyse big data (see Table 4.10.).

Having such capabilities at their disposal, tax administrations that use big data for analytical purposes reported using it, for example, to improve compliance (89%), identify trends (79%) and forecast revenue (64%). Around 70% of tax administrations also indicated using artificial intelligence as part of this analysis. (See Table 4.11.)

Table 4.11. Use of big data for analytical purposes, 2024

Percent of administrations that have the respective process in place

	If yes, ...						
	Big data use cases						
Big data used for analytical purposes	Improve compliance	Identify trends	Policy forecasting	Revenue forecasting	Provide new services	Other purposes	Artificial intelligence / machine learning used as part of the big data analysis
87.0	89.4	78.7	51.1	63.8	55.3	23.4	72.3

Source: (OECD et al., 2024[2]), Inventory of Tax Technology Initiatives, https://www.oecd.org/content/oecd/en/data/datasets/inventory-of-tax-technology-initiatives.html (accessed on 7 February 2025).

Understanding the importance of the use of analytics, the OECD's Forum on Tax Administration developed the *Analytics Maturity Model* (OECD, 2022[5]) to help tax administrations self-assess their current level of maturity in their analytics usage and capability. This provides insight into their current status by identifying areas of weaknesses as well as strengths. As Figure 4.1. shows, it has been completed by over 40 tax administrations, and the results of this are guiding and supporting administrations in their analytics strategies.

Figure 4.1. Analytics Maturity Model self-assessments results

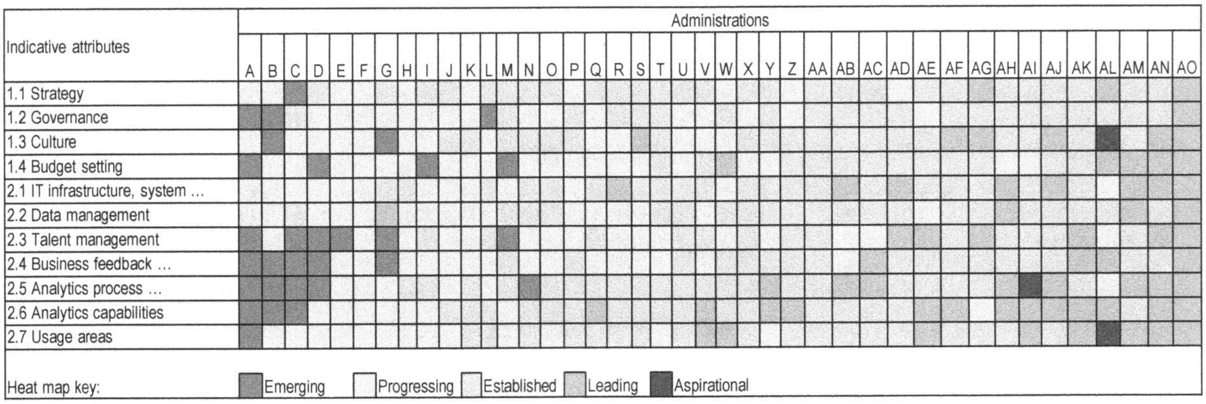

Source: OECD (2022), Analytics Maturity Model, https://www.oecd.org/content/dam/oecd/en/topics/policy-issues/tax-administration/analytics-maturity-model.pdf (accessed on 12 February 2025).

Innovations

Given the increasing importance of the role of data in tax administration and the importance of keeping up with technological advancements, tax administrations are also looking at new and innovative approaches as to how they store, manage and use data.

Table 4.12. illustrates some of those approaches, including the use of network analysis (72%), machine learning (61%), robotic process automation (54%), and cloud storage (52%).

Table 4.12. Innovative approaches used as part of data management activities, 2024

Percent of administrations that have the respective process in place

Cloud storage	Robotic process automation	Machine learning	Network analysis	DataOps approach
51.9	53.7	61.1	72.2	35.2

Source: (OECD et al., 2024[2]), Inventory of Tax Technology Initiatives, https://www.oecd.org/content/oecd/en/data/datasets/inventory-of-tax-technology-initiatives.html (accessed on 7 February 2025).

References

OECD (2024), *Tax Administration 2024: Comparative Information on OECD and other Advanced and Emerging Economies*, OECD Publishing, Paris, https://doi.org/10.1787/2d5fba9c-en. [4]

OECD (2022), *Anaytics Maturity Model*, OECD, Paris, https://www.oecd.org/content/dam/oecd/en/topics/policy-issues/tax-administration/analytics-maturity-model.pdf (accessed on 12 February 2025). [5]

OECD (2022), *Tax Administration 3.0 and Connecting with Natural Systems: Initial Findings*, OECD Publishing, Paris, https://doi.org/10.1787/53b8dade-en. [3]

OECD (2022), *Tax Administration 3.0 and Electronic Invoicing: Initial Findings*, OECD Publishing, Paris, https://doi.org/10.1787/2ffc88ed-en. [6]

OECD (2020), *Tax Administration 3.0: The Digital Transformation of Tax Administration*, OECD Publishing, Paris, https://doi.org/10.1787/ca274cc5-en. [1]

OECD et al. (2024), *Inventory of Tax Technology Initiatives*, https://www.oecd.org/content/oecd/en/data/datasets/inventory-of-tax-technology-initiatives.html (accessed on 7 February 2025). [2]

Note

[1] The OECD report *Tax Administration 3.0 and Electronic Invoicing: Initial Findings* (OECD, 2022[6]) contains information on electronic invoicing systems and some considerations that administrations exploring possible implementation or reform of such systems may wish to take into account.

5 Tax rule management and application

Underlying the future vision of tax administration, as described in the 2020 report *Tax Administration 3.0: The Digital Transformation of Tax Administration* (OECD, 2020[1]), is a shift away from tax rules and calculations being conducted and finalised within the tax administration's IT environment, to moving the rules and relevant information for tax processing into the taxpayers' natural systems. This is already seen in many jurisdictions in pay-as-you-earn systems for salaried employees where taxation processes are integrated into the payroll systems used by employers.

With tax systems being complex, tax administrations are increasingly leveraging technology to streamline processes and improve accuracy. For example, more tax administrations are now making use of machine-readable law. This allows legislation to be encoded in a structured digital format that can be processed by the software systems used in taxpayers' natural systems. This facilitates automated tax calculations, real-time compliance checks, and seamless integration with business and financial systems.

Adopting machine-readable tax rules in appropriate cases can enhance transparency, reduce errors, and improve taxpayer services, while also enabling quicker legislation and policy updates. It can also help to avoid uncertain or inconsistent interpretation of tax legislation. As can be seen in Table 5.1., governments are at different points regarding the use of machine-readable tax law, with around 30% indicating that they publish all tax law in machine-readable format and another 15% indicating that they do this for some tax laws.

Table 5.1. Machine-readable tax law, 2024

Government publishes tax law in machine-readable format		
Yes, for all tax laws	Yes, for some tax laws	No
31.5	14.8	53.7

Source: (OECD et al., 2024[2]), Inventory of Tax Technology Initiatives, https://www.oecd.org/content/oecd/en/data/datasets/inventory-of-tax-technology-initiatives.html (accessed on 7 February 2025).

The remainder of this chapter looks at advances in tax rule management, including the use of assurance frameworks to validate the integration of tax rules into third party products and systems, the automation of registration processes, and the role of artificial intelligence.

Assurance frameworks

Alongside improvements in technology and the wide-spread use of software products, an increasing number of third parties is developing software products for tax purposes. To ensure the integrity of the tax system, to build trust and to assist users with selecting the right products, many tax administrations have put in place some form of assurance mechanism. Those mechanisms are meant to ensure that the third-party products apply tax laws in a consistent manner and deliver outputs that can be accepted by the administration.

As can be seen in Table 5.2., around one third of administrations have a dedicated assurance framework, and the vast majority of those that do not have a framework have implemented other mechanisms to ensure that third-party software packages incorporate tax rules correctly:

- 80% of administrations provide technical documentation to enable product development by software providers;
- 77% of administrations implement controls around the authorisation and validation of information sent or received from those software products; and
- 17% of administrations require software providers to follow set requirements in regard to software development cycles.

Only around 6% have no assurance framework or other mechanism.

Table 5.2. Assurance frameworks, 2024

Percent of administrations that have the respective process in place

Assurance framework exists that allows 3rd parties to incorporate tax rules in their software packages and deliver outputs based on those rules that are accepted by the tax administration	Types of approaches taken by the administration where an assurance framework does **not** exist				
	Administration provides technical documentation to enable product development by software providers	Administration enforces a software development lifecycle that a software provider must follow to meet set requirements	Administration implements controls around authorisation and validation of information sent / received	Other approaches	No approach
35.2	80.0	17.1	77.1	8.6	5.7

Source: (OECD et al., 2024[2]), Inventory of Tax Technology Initiatives, https://www.oecd.org/content/oecd/en/data/datasets/inventory-of-tax-technology-initiatives.html (accessed on 7 February 2025).

Using trustworthy and reliable and secure software products is key to maintaining trust in the automation of tax rule management. As part of this, some administrations are being increasingly transparent about the software products they approve or recognise.

Table 5.3. shows that a third of administrations publish the names of approved or recognised software products. Around 40% of administrations maintain a register of approved or recognised software products, with slightly more than two thirds of these being public. The table also shows that there are different types of approvals or recognition processes, with the majority of tax administrations using a certification process. Of those that use a certification process, over half have their own certification process, and 18% rely on the certification processes of another government body. Other approaches include an administration endorsement of a private certification process (18%), and a process of self-declaration with the administration then conducting random checks (23%).

Table 5.3. Approved or recognised software products, 2024

Percent of administrations that have the respective process in place

Names of approved or recognised software products published	Register of approved or recognised software products maintained		If yes, type of approval or recognition process				
	Register exists	If yes, register is public	Certification by the administration	Certification by another government body	Administration endorsement of a private certification process	Self-declaration with administration conducting random checks	Other approaches
33.3	40.7	68.2	54.5	18.2	18.2	22.7	31.8

Source: (OECD et al., 2024[2]), Inventory of Tax Technology Initiatives, https://www.oecd.org/content/oecd/en/data/datasets/inventory-of-tax-technology-initiatives.html (accessed on 7 February 2025).

Automated registration and deregistration

Taxpayer registration and identification is a key element of an effective tax system as it ensures compliance, enhances trust and transparency, and in some cases can also facilitate access to benefits and grants. It forms the basis for supporting core elements of tax administration work such assessment processes, withholding tax regimes, and third-party reporting and matching.

Automating this process, or parts of it, is an important element of the Tax Administration 3.0 vision (OECD, 2020[1]). Automated registration (and deregistration) at certain events in the taxpayer lifecycle, such as registering a business or registering as a seller on a gig and sharing economy platform, can reduce administrative burdens, increase efficiency and enhance accuracy, while ensuring compliance and building trust.

Table 5.4. illustrates that two thirds of tax administrations can automatically register taxpayers based on data received from third parties, while half can also automatically deregister taxpayers. Some tax systems go further and already allow third parties to automatically register or deregisters taxpayers. However, in most cases this must be with the taxpayer's consent. Only very few administrations can register or deregister taxpayers without their consent.

Table 5.4. Automated registration and deregistration of taxpayers, 2024

Percent of administrations that have the respective process in place

Based on data received from third parties, administration automatically ...		Third party stakeholders can automatically ...			
		Register taxpayers ...		Deregister taxpayers ...	
Registers taxpayers	Deregisters taxpayers	Without taxpayer consent	Only with taxpayer consent	Without taxpayer consent	Only with taxpayer consent
66.7	50.0	3.7	29.6	1.9	20.4

Source: (OECD et al., 2024[2]), Inventory of Tax Technology Initiatives, https://www.oecd.org/content/oecd/en/data/datasets/inventory-of-tax-technology-initiatives.html (accessed on 7 February 2025).

Third party withholding

Withholding regimes support overall tax compliance while significantly reducing burdens for large numbers of taxpayers. This is particularly the case where taxpayers do not need to engage in any post-payment adjustments, for example, where the withholding payment is final or calculated on the correct tax position of the individual taxpayer. This will often require that third parties are provided with information on changes to taxpayer's individual tax positions so as to be able to withhold the correct amount. As can be seen in Table 5.5. slightly over 20% of tax administrations are now providing such information on an automatic basis.

Table 5.5. Third party withholding of taxes, 2024

Percent of administrations that have the respective process in place

Administration automatically provides information on changes to taxpayer's individual tax positions to third parties to facilitate withholding of taxes	If yes, ...			
	Third parties calculate the withholding based on ...		Withholding is done as a result of ...	
	A flat tax rate	The individual tax position	Legislative requirements	Voluntary arrangements
22.2	41.7	58.3	91.7	8.3

Source: (OECD et al., 2024[2]), Inventory of Tax Technology Initiatives, https://www.oecd.org/content/oecd/en/data/datasets/inventory-of-tax-technology-initiatives.html (accessed on 7 February 2025).

Artificial intelligence

Artificial intelligence (AI) is being increasingly used by tax administrations to enhance effectiveness and efficiency within the administration, for example on compliance management, and to improve taxpayer services, including through the development of more real-time and personalised processes for interactions with taxpayers. The data from the *Inventory of Tax Technology Initiatives* shows that 72% of tax administrations use AI (OECD et al., 2024[2]).

There are a range of uses for AI by tax administrations, as can be seen in Table 5.6. The most common is using AI to detect tax evasion and fraud, which is done by three quarters of tax administrations. Other common use cases include as part of risk assessment processes (64%), virtual assistants (59%), aiding officials in making administrative decisions (44%), and making recommendations for actions (41%). Less common uses include ensuring the integrity of tax administration systems/processes (15%), automated provision of personalised information to stakeholders (13%) and dispute resolution (3%). The survey underlying the *Inventory of Tax Technology Initiatives* (OECD et al., 2024[2]) also asked whether administrations use AI to make final administrative decisions, but none indicated that AI is used in this way.

Table 5.6. Artificial intelligence: Main use cases, 2024

Percent of administrations that use artificial intelligence and have the respective process in place

Automated provision of personalised information to stakeholders	Virtual assistants	Risk assessment processes	Detection of tax evasion and fraud	Assistance of tax officials in making administrative decisions	Making recommendations for actions	Dispute resolution	To ensure the integrity of tax administration systems / processes	Other use cases
12.8	59.0	64.1	74.4	43.6	41.0	2.6	15.4	30.8

Note: Percentages relate to the 72% of administrations that indicated using artificial intelligence.
Source: (OECD et al., 2024[2]), Inventory of Tax Technology Initiatives, https://www.oecd.org/content/oecd/en/data/datasets/inventory-of-tax-technology-initiatives.html (accessed on 7 February 2025).

However, whilst AI undoubtedly has many benefits for tax administrations, its adoption must be carefully managed to mitigate risks around ethical challenges, data privacy and bias. Table 5.7. highlights that a large majority of administrations that use AI (87%) have put limitations in place on its use, and around 40% have an ethical framework regarding the use and application of AI.

Table 5.7. Artificial intelligence: Limitations and ethical framework, 2024

Percent of administrations that use artificial intelligence and have the respective process in place

Limitations exist on the use of artificial intelligence	Ethical framework for the application of artificial intelligence exists
87.2	41.0

Note: Percentages relate to the 72% of administrations that indicated using artificial intelligence.
Source: (OECD et al., 2024[2]), Inventory of Tax Technology Initiatives, https://www.oecd.org/content/oecd/en/data/datasets/inventory-of-tax-technology-initiatives.html (accessed on 7 February 2025).

One of the biggest risks regarding the use of AI is ensuring that it remains objective, with administrations putting various processes in place to ensure this. These processes can either be carried out by the tax administration or by a third party, with Table 5.8. providing a breakdown by approach. The table shows that over 80% of administrations indicated that they themselves carry out reviews of AI input information, the probing and testing of AI responses, and the monitoring of AI outputs. The review of the AI source code is done by half of tax administrations.

Table 5.8. Artificial intelligence: Ensuring objectivity, 2024

Percent of administrations that use artificial intelligence and have the respective process in place

Body that carries out the approaches	Approaches taken by the administration to ensure that decisions by the artificial intelligence are objective				
	Reviewing of AI source code	Reviewing of AI input information	Probing and testing of AI responses	Monitoring of AI outputs	Other approaches
Administration	51.3	82.1	84.6	82.1	30.8
Third party	5.1	10.3	10.3	5.1	12.8

Note: Percentages relate to the 72% of administrations that indicated using artificial intelligence.
Source: (OECD et al., 2024[2]), Inventory of Tax Technology Initiatives, https://www.oecd.org/content/oecd/en/data/datasets/inventory-of-tax-technology-initiatives.html (accessed on 7 February 2025).

Innovations

With the management and application of tax rules being automated to a large extent and with vast amounts of data being internally and externally generated, tax administrations continue to look at new and innovative approaches to reduce burdens, provide certainty and ensure compliance.

Table 5.9. highlights some of those innovative approaches. For example:

- 85% of administrations are working with IT systems that automatically identify errors or inconsistencies in the data provided by stakeholders;
- Around 40% of administrations enable the taxpayer or business to test upfront the expected tax treatments of particular scenarios to inform their decision making and allow them to understand their future tax liabilities; and
- Close to 10% of administrations have started using Distributed Ledger Technology in their taxation processes.

Table 5.9. Innovative approaches used as part of tax rule management, 2024

Percent of administrations that have the respective process in place

IT systems are in place that automatically (i.e. without human intervention) identify errors or inconsistencies in the data provided by stakeholders	IT system enable the taxpayer or business to test upfront tax treatments of scenarios to inform their decision making and liabilities	Distributed Ledger Technology (DLT)	
		DLT used in administration's taxation processes	If yes, administration uses smart contracts embedded within DLT
85.2	42.6	9.3	60.0

Source: (OECD et al., 2024[2]), Inventory of Tax Technology Initiatives, https://www.oecd.org/content/oecd/en/data/datasets/inventory-of-tax-technology-initiatives.html (accessed on 7 February 2025).

References

OECD (2020), *Tax Administration 3.0: The Digital Transformation of Tax Administration*, OECD Publishing, Paris, https://doi.org/10.1787/ca274cc5-en. [1]

OECD et al. (2024), *Inventory of Tax Technology Initiatives*, https://www.oecd.org/content/oecd/en/data/datasets/inventory-of-tax-technology-initiatives.html (accessed on 7 February 2025). [2]

6 New skill sets

As reported in the OECD publication *Tax Administration 2024* (OECD, 2024[1]), salary costs of tax administrations average more than 70% of the operating budgets, meaning that the staff and their skills are at the centre of any digital transformation process. Over the past years, the staff usage by function has remained stable with the "Audit, investigation and other verification" function and the "Registration, services, returns and payment processing" function each employing on average 30% of staff, followed by the "Debt collection" function with on average around 10% of staff (see Figure 6.1.).

Figure 6.1. Staff usage by function, 2022

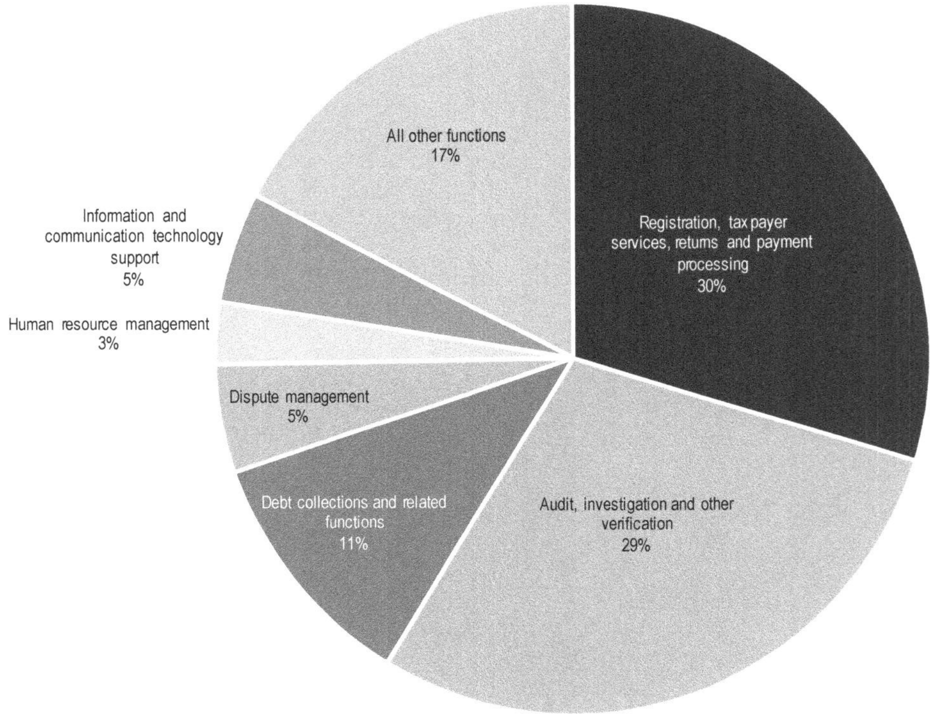

Source: OECD (2024), Tax Administration 2024: Comparative Information on OECD and other Advanced and Emerging Economies, https://doi.org/10.1787/2d5fba9c-en.

However, even though those figures have remained stable for some time, there have already been significant changes with administrations investing in new skills to support e-administration, provide new services and build-up data and analytical capabilities.

This shift towards new skills will expand even further and probably also accelerate with digital transformation. As digital platforms and technology, such as artificial intelligence, become more prevalent in the work of tax administrations, existing staff will need to develop technical expertise in a range of areas, from data analytics to cyber security, and/or new staff with those skills will need to be hired. As mentioned in the 2020 Tax Administration 3.0 report "The skills required will be more focussed on supporting the operation and evolution of the tax administration system as a whole. This will require an expansion in the number of IT professionals, programmers, data scientists, behavioural scientists and strategists." (OECD, 2020[2])

It is against this background that this chapter takes a closer look at tax administrations' approaches towards skill identification and mapping. It also provides information on tax administrations' approaches towards building a digital culture internally and externally.

Skill identification and mapping

For a successful digital transformation, tax administrations may wish to consider identifying and mapping both the future skills that will be required, and the current capabilities of staff within the administration.

Table 6.1. shows there is mixed progress on this. Slightly more than a quarter of administrations have identified the future skills required for a successful digital transformation for the whole administration, and an additional 45% have done this for parts of the administration. Of those, only slightly more than half (59%) also map the skills of their current staff against the skills that are required. Interestingly, of those that perform the mapping exercise, there is very strong support for ensuring the mapping outcomes are reviewed on a regular basis and also reflected in the wider HR strategy. This may suggest that for those who carry out the mapping, it is a very useful exercise.

Table 6.1. Skills for digital transformation: Identification and mapping, 2024

Percent of administrations that have the respective process in place

Identification of future skills for a successful digital transformation		If yes (for whole or parts of the administration) ...			
		Skills of officials are mapped against skills that are required	If yes, ...		
For the whole administration	For parts of the administration		Mapping covers a multi-year period	Mapping is reviewed on a regular basis	Mapping outcomes are reflected in the wider HR strategy
27.8	44.4	59.0	87.0	91.3	100.0

Source: (OECD et al., 2024[3]), Inventory of Tax Technology Initiatives, https://www.oecd.org/content/oecd/en/data/datasets/inventory-of-tax-technology-initiatives.html (accessed on 7 February 2025).

Skill identification and mapping can be complex processes, which is why roughly a quarter of administrations that have identified the future skills needed for a successful digital transformation (for the whole administrations or for parts of it) indicated using an external supplier, such as a consultancy firm, for both exercises (see Table 6.2.).

The drive for digital transformation is not unique to tax administrations, but something that other government organisations and external partners also grapple with. Therefore, it can make sense to collaborate on common issues, as demonstrated in Table 6.2. Of those administrations that have identified the future skills needed, three quarters collaborate with other government organisations and external partners to improve the staff skills required for digital transformation, and slightly more than 40% collaborate with those bodies on a potential recruitment pool for digital transformation.

Table 6.2. Skills for digital transformation: Use of external suppliers and collaboration, 2024

Percent of administrations that have the respective process in place

External supplier, such as a consultancy firm, conducted ...		Collaboration with other government organisations or external partners ...	
The identification of future skills required	The mapping of skills that officials currently have	To improve staff skills required for digital transformation	For a potential recruitment pool for digital transformation
28.2	25.6	74.4	43.6

Note: Percentages relate to administrations that have identified the future skills needed for a successful digital transformation either for the whole administrations or for parts of it (see Table 6.1.).
Source: (OECD et al., 2024[3]), Inventory of Tax Technology Initiatives, https://www.oecd.org/content/oecd/en/data/datasets/inventory-of-tax-technology-initiatives.html (accessed on 7 February 2025).

To assist administrations with understanding their maturity regarding human resources (HR) management, the OECD's Forum on Tax Administration developed a Human Resources Maturity Model, which highlights elements that are important for implementing and maintaining good HR practices, including strategy setting and governance processes, workforce planning and management, and staff support. (OECD, 2025[4])

Digital culture

Transforming the organisational culture of the tax administration is a core element of success for digital transformation. This includes communicating the high-level vision of digital transformation and the benefits it can bring to the administration, the taxpayers, and the wider society.

Understanding that building a digital culture is a process that might require breaking old habits and implementing new methods, taking a strategic approach might be beneficial. Around two thirds of administrations report having developed a strategy to build a digital culture within their organisation. Moreover, close to half of the administrations have done the same with respect to their taxpayer community, and 40% with respect to their advisor community. (See Table 6.3.)

As mentioned, communication is important for success, particularly to maintain buy-in, which is why:

- Two thirds of administrations ensure their digital transformation strategy is communicated to all staff so that they understand their roles and responsibilities; and
- Three quarters of administrations regularly update staff and other key stakeholders on the implementation and progress of the digital transformation strategy. (See Table 6.3.)

Table 6.3. Digital culture: Strategy, communication and engagement, 2024

Percent of administrations that have the respective process in place

Strategy developed to build a digital culture within the ...			The digital transformation strategy or changes are communicated to all officials so that they understand their individual roles and responsibilities	Staff and other stakeholders are regularly engaged on the digital transformation strategy, its implementation and progress
Administration	Taxpayer community	Advisor community		
66.7	48.1	40.7	66.7	75.9

Source: (OECD et al., 2024[3]), Inventory of Tax Technology Initiatives, https://www.oecd.org/content/oecd/en/data/datasets/inventory-of-tax-technology-initiatives.html (accessed on 7 February 2025).

More information on the importance of transforming the organisational culture and adopting an innovative and taxpayer-centric mindset throughout the organisation, including recommended actions and case studies, can be found in the report *Tax Administration 3.0 - From Vision to Strategy* (OECD, 2025[5]).

References

OECD (2025), *Human Resources Maturity Model*, OECD, Paris, http://www.oecd.org/content/dam/oecd/en/topics/policy-issues/tax-administration/human-resources-maturity-model.pdf (accessed on 27 May 2025). [4]

OECD (2025), *Tax Administration 3.0 - From Vision to Strategy*, OECD, Paris, http://www.oecd.org/content/dam/oecd/en/topics/policy-issues/tax-administration/tax-administration-3-0-from-vision-to-strategy.pdf. [5]

OECD (2024), *Tax Administration 2024: Comparative Information on OECD and other Advanced and Emerging Economies*, OECD Publishing, Paris, https://doi.org/10.1787/2d5fba9c-en. [1]

OECD (2020), *Tax Administration 3.0: The Digital Transformation of Tax Administration*, OECD Publishing, Paris, https://doi.org/10.1787/ca274cc5-en. [2]

OECD et al. (2024), *Inventory of Tax Technology Initiatives*, https://www.oecd.org/content/oecd/en/data/datasets/inventory-of-tax-technology-initiatives.html (accessed on 7 February 2025). [3]

7 Governance frameworks

Embedding digital transformation into the core governance and processes of the tax administration is important to help to ensure that longer-term transformation is considered alongside other short-term priorities. Digital transformation also necessitates the joining-up of systems and processes across multiple stakeholders, including private and public sector stakeholders domestically and internationally. Having a governance framework can help to bring together those stakeholders in a structured manner and thus assist tax administrations with establishing clear decision-making processes, guidelines, and defined roles and responsibilities to effectively implement and oversee digital transformation initiatives.

There are different ways of implementing governance frameworks and the approaches may vary according to an administration's unique context and needs. At its core, though, it will involve the administration setting objectives for the digital transformation, alongside a number of strategic actions that can be taken to achieve these objectives, as well as defining the way stakeholders co-operate. This chapter examines how tax administrations approach digital transformation and the strategies and governance features that they have put in place.

Digital transformation strategy

Digital transformation represents a fundamental change in the operating model for an organisation, and for large and complex organisations such as tax administrations this can only happen incrementally. To provide for a structured approach, many administrations are increasingly developing digital transformation strategies that set out objectives and plan the timing and priority of the incremental steps.

To support tax administrations with determining possible pathways it may wish to follow in its digital transformation journey, the OECD's Forum on Tax Administration (FTA) created a *Digital Transformation Maturity Model* (OECD, 2022[1]) which is available in four languages. The model is a self-assessment tool that can help organisations understand their current level of digital maturity and, by setting out the pathway for higher levels of maturity, can help inform digital transformation strategies and identify target areas for improvement. The model has been completed by almost 60 tax administrations. The assessment results, published in the form of an anonymised heat map (see Figure 7.1. for the latest results), also allow tax administrations to compare themselves with peers and to reach out, through the FTA Secretariat, for peer-to-peer discussion and learning purposes. (OECD, 2022[1])

Figure 7.1. Digital Transformation Maturity Model self-assessment results

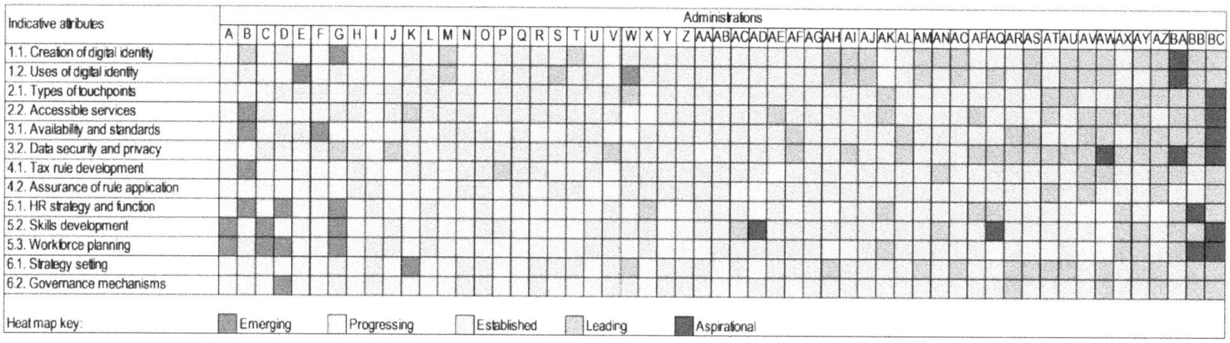

Source: OECD (2022), Digital Transformation Maturity Mode, https://www.oecd.org/content/dam/oecd/en/topics/policy-issues/tax-administration/digital-transformation-maturity-model.pdf (accessed on 12 February 2025).

The importance of digital transformation strategies is evident when looking at Table 7.1. which illustrates that nearly 80% of administrations have developed a digital transformation strategy. Of those that have, close to 70% of administrations reported having strategies that last 3-5 years, with the remaining administrations having strategies with shorter (9%) or longer-term timeframes (21%).

Table 7.1. also confirms that tax administrations recognise the importance of monitoring the progress of their digital transformation strategy, with the vast majority of administrations doing so. There is also value in administrations considering whether and how they should participate in a wider digital transformation strategy of the government. This may help provide joined-up government services in the future, reduce costs through economies of scale, and avoid duplication of efforts. As shown in Table 7.1., virtually all administrations align their digital transformation strategy to the government's wider digital transformation strategy. Finally, having ring-fenced funding for the duration of the strategy may also be something administrations want to consider to ensure its sustainability, with just under half of administrations doing so.

Table 7.1. Digital transformation strategy features, 2024

Percent of administrations that have the respective process in place

Digital transformation strategy developed	Time frame of the strategy			Progress against the digital transformation strategy is monitored	If yes, ... Funding is ring-fenced for the duration of the strategy	Government has a wider digital transformation strategy	If yes, ... Administration's strategy has been aligned to the government's wider digital transformation strategy
	Less than 3 years	3 to 5 years	More than 5 years				
79.6	9.3	69.8	20.9	95.3	48.8	97.7	97.6

Source: (OECD et al., 2024[2]), Inventory of Tax Technology Initiatives, https://www.oecd.org/content/oecd/en/data/datasets/inventory-of-tax-technology-initiatives.html (accessed on 7 February 2025).

Digital transformation affects all parts of an administration as well as a broad range of stakeholders, including taxpayers, intermediaries, service providers and policy makers. To ensure success, administrations may wish to involve those stakeholders already during the development of the strategy. As can be seen in Table 7.2., nearly all administrations (98%) that have a digital transformation strategy have involved all relevant internal stakeholders, and a significant amount (86%) have sought input from external stakeholders. Making use of data and analytical tools, just over half of administrations have forecast different scenarios during the process of drawing up the strategy.

Table 7.2. Digital transformation strategy development, 2024

Administrations that have the respective process in place as a percent of those that have a digital transformation strategy

All key internal stakeholders, including senior management and relevant functional areas, involved in drawing-up the strategy	Input sought from external stakeholders, such as other parts of government, tax policy makers, taxpayer bodies and representatives	Data analysis and analytics used to forecast different scenarios during the process of drawing-up the strategy
97.7	86.0	53.5

Note: Percentages relate to administrations that have developed a digital transformation strategy (see Table 7.1.).
Source: (OECD et al., 2024[2]), Inventory of Tax Technology Initiatives, https://www.oecd.org/content/oecd/en/data/datasets/inventory-of-tax-technology-initiatives.html (accessed on 7 February 2025).

Digital transformation governance

An important part of governance frameworks is having a governance body to oversee the relevant processes, provide strategic direction, and ensure the smooth implementation of the recommended actions laid out in the digital transformation strategy.

Table 7.3. outlines that close to 80% of administrations have a senior management governance body in place to oversee the digital transformation of the administration. Of these, nearly half have external stakeholders holding formal positions on the governance body. Four fifths of the external stakeholders come from other parts of government, followed by the private sector (35%) and civil society (25%).

Table 7.3. Governance bodies, 2024

Percent of administrations that have the respective process in place

Senior management governance body established to oversee the digital transformation	If yes, ...				
	External stakeholders have formal positions on the governance body	If yes, sectors where external stakeholder come from ...			
		Other parts of government	Private sector	Civil society	Other sectors
77.8	47.6	80.0	35.0	25.0	15.0

Source: (OECD et al., 2024[2]), Inventory of Tax Technology Initiatives, https://www.oecd.org/content/oecd/en/data/datasets/inventory-of-tax-technology-initiatives.html (accessed on 7 February 2025).

In addition to governance bodies, there are other relevant governance features and processes that administrations may have in place, as set out in Table 7.4. For example, around 80% of administrations have programme-management activities adopted to support the transition to a digital tax administration, and 70% have specific positions in place to manage and lead the work on digital transformation, such as a chief digital officer.

It is also interesting to see that where governments have a whole of government approach to digital transformation governance, slightly more than 60% of administrations are directly represented in such governance structures, a clear sign of the importance of tax administration to wider digital transformation within a jurisdiction.

Table 7.4. Other selected governance features, 2024

Percent of administrations that have the respective process in place

Programme-management activities adopted that support transitioning to a digital tax administration	Specific roles / positions in place to manage and lead the work on digital transformation, e.g. a chief digital officer	Government has a whole of government approach to digital transformation governance	If yes, ... Administration is directly represented in the governance structures of the whole of government approach
81.5	70.4	72.2	61.5

Source: (OECD et al., 2024[2]), Inventory of Tax Technology Initiatives, https://www.oecd.org/content/oecd/en/data/datasets/inventory-of-tax-technology-initiatives.html (accessed on 7 February 2025).

Understanding the importance of setting a digital transformation strategy and having the proper governance structures in place, the OECD published a new report *Tax Administration 3.0 - From Vision to Strategy* (OECD, 2025[3]). This report describes the actions that Commissioners and senior leaders can take in order to develop and operationalise a digital transformation strategy. It covers organisational change and how administrations operate internally, as well as how they engage with the wider tax ecosystem. It also contains several links to presentations on actions already being taken by different administrations in order to provide inspiration for possible new initiatives.

References

OECD (2025), *Tax Administration 3.0 - From Vision to Strategy*, OECD, Paris, http://www.oecd.org/content/dam/oecd/en/topics/policy-issues/tax-administration/tax-administration-3-0-from-vision-to-strategy.pdf. [3]

OECD (2022), *Digital Transformation Maturity Model*, OECD, Paris, https://www.oecd.org/content/dam/oecd/en/topics/policy-issues/tax-administration/digital-transformation-maturity-model.pdf (accessed on 12 February 2025). [1]

OECD et al. (2024), *Inventory of Tax Technology Initiatives*, https://www.oecd.org/content/oecd/en/data/datasets/inventory-of-tax-technology-initiatives.html (accessed on 7 February 2025). [2]

www.ingramcontent.com/pod-product-compliance
Lightning Source LLC
LaVergne TN
LVHW081740071126
851857LV00041B/1848